top
italian
wines
1997

top italian wines 1997

Editor in Chief
Stefano Bonilli

Wine Editor
Daniele Cernilli

Articles Editor
Linda Parkoff

Graphic Design
Fabio Cremonesi

Send correspondence to
GAMBERO ROSSO
U.S. Office
225 Lafayette St., Suite 1213
New York, NY 10012
Phone: 212-334 8499, Fax: 212-334 9173

European Office
53 Via Arenula
00186 Rome, Italy, Phone: 39-6-68300741
Fax: 39-6-6877217

e-mail: 74644.2162@compuserve.com
or gambero@tol.it

Gambero Rosso Inc.
Publisher & President
Stefano Bonilli

Printed in Italy
November 1996
Baioni Stampa Srl
Via A. Bertoloni, 26/b - Roma

CONTENTS

94   This number refers to the wine's score based on a 100 point scale

FOREWORD

*S*ave this book. You'll find our tasting notes for the 96 best Italian wines released during 1996 and 1997 in this little volume. Although many of these wines have famous names, some are made by small producers who one day will be known throughout the world. Our book will help you discover this new talent along with us. Ratings are based on a hundred-point scale, as is customary in international tastings, and this is our list of the highest scorers. They come from many wine producing zones of Italy, but especially from Piedmont and Tuscany, the two most important Italian regions for top quality wines. But other areas are also represented, some of them very famous and very productive such as the Veneto, Sicily, and Lombardy, and others in their first appearances on the world stage, such as the Marches, Umbria and the Abruzzi.

Almost every corner of the Italian peninsula is marvelously well-suited for grape-growing and wine making, and not just a few small and very special areas, as in other countries. The number of local varieties of grapes used for wine making is vast: it ranges from Nebbiolo and Barbera - Piedmontese reds - to Tuscan Sangiovese, to Verdicchio in the Marches, and to Nero d'Avola in Sicily.

But the classic international varieties of French origin, such as Cabernet Sauvignon, Merlot, Pinot Noir, Chardonnay and Sauvignon Blanc have also found favor in virtually all the major grape-growing zones, from the northern mountains of Alto Adige to the Mediterranean terrain of Sicily. Our top-scoring wines give only a peek into the immense panorama of Italian winemaking. It is based on ancient traditions dating back thousands of years.

With this booklet in hand, our readers can see for themselves: the notion that Italian wine is simply cheap and cheerful is long outdated. The truth is that the best Italian wines are also among the best wines in the world.

OVERVIEW OF THE YEARS
1970 TO 1993

	BARBARESCO	BRUNELLO DI MONTALCINO	BAROLO	CHIANTI CLASSICO	VINO NOBILE DI MONTEPULCIANO	AMARONE
1970	●●●●	●●●●	●●●●	●●●●●	●●●●	●●●●
1971	●●●●	●●●	●●●●●	●●●●●	●●●●	●●●●
1972	●	●	●	●●	●	●
1973	●●	●●●	●●	●●	●●●	●●
1974	●●●●	●●	●●●●	●●●	●●●	●●●●
1975	●●	●●●●●	●●	●●●●	●●●●	●●●
1976	●●	●	●●	●●	●●	●●●●
1977	●●	●●●	●●	●●●●	●●●●	●●●
1978	●●●●●	●●●●	●●●●●	●●●●●	●●●●●	●●●
1979	●●●●	●●●●	●●●●	●●●●	●●●●	●●●●
1980	●●●●	●●●●	●●●●	●●●●	●●	●●●
1981	●●●	●●●	●●●	●●●	●●●	●●●

	poor	●
mediocre	●●
average	●●●
very good	●●●●
excellent	●●●●●

	BARBARESCO	BRUNELLO DI MONTALCINO	BAROLO	CHIANTI CLASSICO	VINO NOBILE DI MONTEPULCIANO	AMARONE
1982	●●●●●	●●●●●	●●●●●	●●●●	●●●●	●
1983	●●●●	●●●●	●●●●	●●●●	●●●●	●●●●●
1984	●	●●	●●	●	●	●●
1985	●●●●●	●●●●●	●●●●●	●●●●●	●●●●●	●●●●
1986	●●●	●●●	●●●	●●●●	●●●●	●●●
1987	●●	●●	●●	●●	●●	●●
1988	●●●●●	●●●●●	●●●●●	●●●●●	●●●●●	●●●●●
1989	●●●●●	●●	●●●●●	●	●	●●
1990	●●●●●	●●●●●	●●●●●	●●●●●	●●●●●	●●●●●
1991	●●●	●●●	●●●	●●●	●●●	●●
1992	●●	●●	●●	●	●	●
1993	●●●	●●●●	●●●	●●●●	●●●●●	●●●●

BAROLO GRAN BUSSIA RISERVA '90

Poderi Aldo Conterno
Monforte d'Alba [Cuneo]
tel. 39-173-78150

A very great Barolo, traditional and innovative at the same time. Immensely powerful, but also elegant and aristocratic. The color is an intense and concentrated garnet. Complex aromas, with hints of violets, raspberries and oak. Exceptionally round and full in the mouth, with obvious but not aggressive tannins. A true masterpiece by the great maestro of Barolo, Aldo Conterno.

98

Imported by Vias
New York, NY

ROSSO GASTALDI '89

Gastaldi
Neive [Cuneo]
tel. 39-173-677400

A unique and astonishing wine. It is made from a variety that has not yet been definitively identified but which probably belongs to the Grenache family. The color is a virtually opaque ruby. Superbly intense aromas, with an exceptional concentration of fruit scents (black currant, sour cherry, raspberry). Incredible concentration in the mouth, remarkable tannins and the clear potential for very long life.

95

Imported by Vindivino
Chicago, IL

LANGHE ROSSO
DARMAGI '93

Angelo Gaja
Barbaresco [Cuneo]
tel. 39-173-635158

*O*ne of the best versions ever of Angelo Gaja's Darmagi. A great red made solely from Cabernet Sauvignon, it resembles the more famous wines of California and Bordeaux, while adhering to the regional character of its own territory, the Langhe. It has a dense ruby color and intense, complex aromas with notes of red berries, graphite, and a hint of spice. The taste is elegant but still shows a full endowment of the tannins that promise a long cellar life.

94

Imported by Vinifera Imports
Ronkonkoma, NY

SEIFILE '93

Fiorenzo Nada
Treiso [Cuneo]
tel. 39-173-638254

*T*his exceptional and rare red produced in Treiso by Fiorenzo Nada is made with the Langhe's most typical mixture of grapes: 80% Barbera and 20% Nebbiolo. The '93 harvest has given us an outstanding version. It is an impressively concentrated wine with a dense ruby color. The nose is fruity with delicate notes of vanilla and toasted oak in the background. Powerful and compact in the mouth, it has excellent tannins and a long, satisfying finish.

94

Imported by Premium Brands Inc.
Forest Hills, NY

BAROLO VIGNA RIÖNDA RISERVA '90

Vigna Riönda di Massolino
Serralunga d'Alba [Cuneo]
tel. 39-173-613138

*B*arolo fans know that some of the most austere and long-lived versions come from Vigna Riönda in Serralunga. This one from the Massolino winery is a superb example of a great traditional Barolo. Its complex and noble aromas have scents of violet, spice and oak. The taste is authoritative and majestic, with rich tannins and a very long finish. A wine that will entrance those who love this type of Barolo.

93

Imported by Winebow
HoHoKus, NJ

SULBRIC '94

Franco M. Martinetti
Torino
tel. 39-11-546634

*M*ade from Barbera and Cabernet Sauvignon, this is one of the most interesting wines we tasted this year. It is produced near Nizza Monferrato by Franco Martinetti, a knowledgeable food enthusiast who is also enthralled by great wine. It is an elegant red with an intense ruby color. Hints of sour cherry, vanilla and toasted oak are woven into its fascinating fragrance. The flavor is full and very delicate, demonstrating an evident search for harmony.

93

Not imported

BARBARESCO
SORÌ TILDÌN '93

Angelo Gaja
Barbaresco [Cuneo]
tel. 39-173-635158

*K*ing Gaja never makes a mistake. Even from a difficult vintage like 1993 he has produced a true masterpiece of harmony and elegance. Its intense ruby color has distinct garnet nuances. Extremely fine aromas show hints of violet, new oak and a touch of toast. The wine is full and balanced in the mouth with sweet, velvety tannin and a memorably lengthy finish.

92

Imported by Vinifera Imports
Ronkonkoma, NY

BARBERA D'ALBA
VIGNA DEI ROMANI '94

Enzo Boglietti
La Morra [Cuneo]
tel. 39-173-50330

*A*n explosion of fragrance and flavor; that is the first impression made by this splendid red. A modern, elegant, yet powerful wine, with intensely fruity, vanilla-laden aromas and a full, lasting taste. Its producer, Enzo Boglietti, a rising star in the winemaking world of La Morra, has some knockout Barolos in store for us in the coming years.

92

Exported by Marc De Grazia
Florence, Italy

BAROLO ESTATE VINEYARD '90

Marchesi di Barolo
Barolo [Cuneo]
tel. 39-173-56101

*C*uriously enough, this winery has chosen to use an English term, "estate vineyard," to explain that this splendid wine is made solely with grapes from its own property. By any name, this is a modern and elegant Barolo. The fine and intense aroma has a light touch of vanilla. The taste is full and harmonious with a very long finish.

Imported by Kobrand
New York, NY

BAROLO RISERVA '90

Pira
Barolo [Cuneo]
tel. 39-173-56108

*W*hen the firm was still owned by Enrico Pira, it produced great old-fashioned country Barolos. This wine, produced by the Borgogno family in consultation with enologist Giorgio Rivetti, is a modern version. Its intense aroma has distinct notes of violets and toasted oak, while its full flavor, although elegant and aristocratic, shows undeniable backbone.

Exported by Marc De Grazia
Florence, Italy

LA VIGNA
DI SONVICO '94

Cascina La Barbatella
Nizza Monferrato [Asti]
tel. 39-141-701434

A small estate, a small miracle. Angelo Sonvico's La Barbatella has forced its way into the elite of great Italian wineries. The Vigna di Sonvico is a blend of Barbera and a small portion of Cabernet Sauvignon. The color is a dark ruby, while the scent presents aromas of black fruits, sour cherries and vanilla. On the palate, the union between the two very different varieties provides a measure of exuberance and backbone. A fine example of a wine that, although already very enjoyable, will certainly have a long life.

92

Not imported

MONPRÀ '94

Conterno Fantino
Monforte d'Alba [Cuneo]
tel. 39-173-78204

*N*ebbiolo, Barbera and small amounts of Cabernet Sauvignon are the grapes used in this delicious and very modern red produced by a winery that we consider one of the most dependable in the entire Langhe zone. The color is an intense, concentrated red and the aromas are powerfully fruity with notes of berries and vanilla. On the palate, the taste is full and balanced, with good tannin.

92

Imported by Empson USA
Alexandria, VA

VIGNA LARIGI '94

Elio Altare
La Morra [Cuneo]
tel. 39-173-50835

*M*aking a wine of great character in a forgettable year is possible only for those who live an intense vineyard life. Elio Altare, an extraordinarily sensitive winemaker, offers us a dazzling version of his Vigna Larigi from the '94 vintage, made solely from Barbera. A magnificent red, it is as elegant and harmonious as those from better years, with elegant scents of oak and vanilla and a full, round flavor.

92

Imported by Vindivino
Chicago, IL

BARBARESCO
BRICH RONCHI '93

Albino Rocca
Barbaresco [Cuneo]
tel. 39-173-635145

*T*his wine is a newcomer, but not a surprise. We've been following the progress of this little winery for years, and we expected a great performance like this from one moment to the next. This Barbaresco '93 from the Brich Ronchi cru is a real showstopper. It displays elegant aromas, with light notes of new oak in the background and a very well balanced taste, not excessively tannic or aggressive.

91

Imported by Michael Skurnik Wines
Syosset, NY

BAROLO PARAFADA RISERVA '90

Vigna Riönda di Massolino
Serralunga d'Alba [Cuneo]
tel. 39-173-613138

*L*ess complex and intense than the Vigna Riönda, but very elegant. Its producer, while respectful of tradition, paid attention to more modern techniques, above all in the use of wood. The resulting Barolo is weighty, but not excessively so, more linear and less austere, with scents of berries and violets against a light background of oak and vanilla. The taste is very round, but without any aggressive tannin.

91

Imported by Winebow
HoHoKus, NJ

MONFERRATO ROSSO PIN '94

La Spinetta
Castagnole Lanze [Asti]
tel. 39-141-877396

*T*his winery is known for a series of excellent Moscatos, but it was hard for Giorgio Rivetti and his brother to suppress the wish to also make an impression with a competitive red. And so they created Pin, a blend of Barbera, Cabernet and Nebbiolo. The percentage of Nebbiolo has increased in the last few years, which has transformed the wine by giving it the austerity, noble tannins and length that are indispensable for proper aging.

91

Imported by Michael Skurnik Wines
Syosset, NY

BARBARESCO
RABAJÀ '93

Bruno Rocca
Barbaresco [Cuneo]
tel. 39-173-635112

*T*he usual Rabajà cru Barbaresco made by Bruno Rocca. The '93 version is again a red of great stature. Delicate aromas of violets and toasted oak with a light note of vanilla in the background. On the palate it is very well-balanced, with sumptuous, smooth tannins. The structure is elegant, although it doesn't have the power of the wines from '89 or '90.

90

Imported by Dufour & Co. Ltd.
North Bergen, NJ

BARBERA D'ALBA
BRICCO MARUN '94

Matteo Correggia
Canale [Cuneo]
tel. 39-173-978009

*M*atteo Correggia is the child prodigy of winemaking in the Roero zone. His wines are always models both of technical perfection and of elegance. Refinement is their ace in the hole since they can't compete in terms of structure with their cousins from the Langhe. But they do win. For example, this Barbera d'Alba Bricco Marun '94, despite an inferior harvest, has delicately fruity aromas with a pleasant note of vanilla. The taste is full and the finish is unusually elegant.

90

Imported by Michael Skurnik Wines
Syosset, NY

BAROLO CANNUBI '92

Paolo Scavino
Castiglione Falletto [Cuneo]
tel. 39-173-62850

*E*nrico Scavino always manages to amaze us. With this Barolo Cannubi '92, he has probably achieved the greatest possible perfection, both technical and viticultural. It is not easy to make a wine like this one from a harvest like that one. And yet, the concentrated color, the elegant - even fruity - aromas, and the powerful, full taste were there to demonstrate that even in a miserable year, you can produce great wines.

Exported by Marc De Grazia
Florence, Italy

BAROLO CIABOT MENTIN GINESTRA '92

Domenico Clerico
Monforte d'Alba [Cuneo]
tel. 39-173-78171

*W*e never expected to find a wine like this from the dreadful harvest of '92. In order to produce this, Domenico Clerico, the legendary winemaker from Monforte, had to be brutally selective in the vineyard, using only grapes capable of giving a result like this one. In fact, the Barolo of the Ciabot Mentin Ginestra '92 cru has a concentrated garnet ruby color, intense aromas with notes of violet and oak, and a full, authoritative flavor with some residual but understandable tannic edges.

Exported by Marc De Grazia
Florence, Italy

LOAZZOLO FORTETO DELLA LUJA
PIASA RISCHEI '93

Forteto della Luja
Loazzolo [Asti]
tel. 39-141-831596

*T*his Moscato Passito, made from late harvest Muscat grapes, comes from the Piedmontese winery that was the first in the region to spotlight this type of wine. It has the warm, deep color of old gold and a very intense fragrance. Its bouquet embodies and enhances the full range of aromatic and floral scents of the variety. The flavor is not cloying but sweet, velvety and full, with a delicate, lightly bitter aftertaste.

90

Imported by Robert Chadderdon Selections
New York, NY

VALENTINO BRUT
ZÉRO '92

Poderi Rocche dei Manzoni
Monforte d'Alba [Cuneo]
tel. 39-173-78421

*T*he first Piedmont spumante ever to reach our top category is produced by Valentino Migliorini in Monforte d'Alba, the heart of Barolo country. Using only Chardonnay grapes, he manages to make a wonderful wine that unites the refined grace of the best Blanc de Blancs and power worthy of the great reds of the zone. It has a brilliant straw-yellow color and very fine bubbles. The fragrance is intense, with a hint of yeast and plum. On the mouth, the wine is full and elegant but assertive.

90

Imported by Robert Chadderdon Selections
New York, NY

FRANCIACORTA CUVÉE ANNAMARIA CLEMENTI '89

Ca' del Bosco
Erbusco [Brescia]
tel. 39-30-7760600

*T*his is one of the highest scores ever attained by an Italian spumante. A splendid wine, made from Chardonnay grapes with the addition of small amounts of Pinot Bianco and Pinot Nero. The grapes are fermented and aged in small oak barrels. The wine is straw-yellow with light golden highlights and extremely fine, long-lasting bubbles. The bouquet is complex, with scents of yeast, vanilla and light but elegant fruity undertones.

96

Imported by Winebow
HoHoKus, NJ

FRANCIACORTA GRAN CUVÉE PAS OPERÉ '91

Bellavista
Erbusco [Brescia]
tel. 39-30-7760276

*T*his firm, owned by Vittorio Moretti, is one of the most important in Italy's wine sector. Among the numerous Bellavista sparkling wines, this Gran Cuvée Pas Operé '91 stands out. It is gold-tinged straw color. The intense, generous bouquet is rich in nuances, with yeast, vanilla, and white flowers predominating. On the palate it is complex, structured and elegant, revealing delicately toasty hints of hazelnuts. The mousse is very fine, the texture creamy. A truly outstanding wine.

92

Imported by Empson USA
Alexandria, VA

FRANCIACORTA
MAGNIFICENTIA

Uberti
Erbusco [Brescia]
tel. 39-30-7267476

*T*his is a non-vintage wine, but it is better than almost all vintage spumanti, and not only those from the Franciacorta zone. Made from Chardonnay grapes, it has the elegance of a great Blanc de Blancs. It is a brilliant straw-yellow and has extremely fine, compact bubbles. The aromas are intensely fruity, with scents resembling plums and ripe pineapple. On the palate, the wine reveals excellent structure and noteworthy balance.

92

Not imported

FRANCIACORTA
DOSAGE ZÉRO '92

Ca' del Bosco
Erbusco [Brescia]
tel. 39-30-7760600

*D*osage Zéro is an Extra Brut made with Chardonnay, Pinot Bianco and Pinot Nero grapes from the 1992 vintage. It was aged on its lees for two and a half years before disgorgement. It has an extremely fine mousse and a creamy texture. The scents of white fruit - particularly plum - and yeast reveal considerable complexity. It is well-constituted, dry, lively and elegant on the palate, with subtle hints of fruit and vanilla.

91

Imported by Winebow
HoHoKus, NY

VALTELLINA SFURSAT
5 STELLE '94

Nino Negri
Chiuro [Sondrio]
tel. 39-342-482521

*T*his is a little jewel from one of the northernmost corners of Italy. It is made from Nebbiolo grapes left to dry on large wooden trays. After vinification, which takes place in January, the wine ages in oak barrels for at least two years. The result is a powerful and austere red of an intense ruby color, with distinct garnet tinges. It has a very intense fragrance with hints of sour cherries preserved in spirits. The taste is dry, full, very smooth and long.

90

Imported by F. Wildman & Sons
New York, NY

ROSSO FAYE '93

Pojer & Sandri
Faedo [Trento]
tel. 39-461-650342

*T*his red made from Merlot, Cabernet and Lagrein grapes really amazed us during our tasting. It is produced by Mario Pojer and Fiorentino Sandri, newcomers to the ranks of our Top Italian Wine producers. Its color is a very concentrated ruby, its aromas are intensely fruity with nuances of berries and vanilla, and its flavor is extraordinarily full and round with sweet, not at all aggressive tannins.

95

Imported by Vindivino
Chicago, IL

SAN LEONARDO '93

Tenuta San Leonardo
Borghetto all'Adige [Trento]
tel. 39-464-689004

*M*ade from a classic Bordeaux Haut Médoc style blend [Cabernet Sauvignon 60% Cabernet Franc 30% Merlot 10%], this red is one of the most interesting innovative wines in Italy and in one of its best-ever versions. Less powerful but more elegant than in '90 and '88, it is a dark and concentrated garnet-tinged ruby. The bouquet is elegant and linear, a herbaceous Cabernet scent together with hints of raspberry and vanilla. The flavor is very intense with some residual but understandable tannic harshness.

95

Imported by Vias
New York, NY

GRANATO '93

Foradori
Mezzolombardo [Trento]
tel. 39-461-601046

*M*ade entirely of Teroldego grapes, this great red is a completely indigenous Italian wine. Elisabetta and Gabriella Foradori produce it with the best grapes from their own vineyards. The dark ruby color, with light garnet nuances, is very concentrated. The scent is intense and fruity, with notes of blackberries and raspberries and hints of vanilla and menthol. On the palate, the wine is powerful but elegant and refined, the tannins compact and sweet, and the length excellent.

93

Imported by Vias
New York, NY

GIULIO FERRARI
RISERVA DEL FONDATORE
BRUT '88

Ferrari
Trento
tel. 39-461-922500

A victorious return for Giulio Ferrari in an '88 version that makes us forget the little uncertainties of the year before. This time we are offered a wonderful and elegant Blanc de Blancs (made solely with Chardonnay grapes). It is a light straw-yellow, with very compact, fine bubbles. The scents are delicately fruity and floral, with light hints of plum, pineapple and breadcrusts. The taste is full, extremely harmonious, and has a very long finish.

92

Imported by Paterno
Chicago, IL

TEROLDEGO ROTALIANO
SGARZON '94

Foradori
Mezzolombardo [Trento]
tel. 39-461-601046

T heir deep respect for the Teroldego variety and the innovative techniques in their winery have led Elisabetta and her mother Gabriella Foradori to produce the best wines in the Trentino region. Lo Sgarzon is a vineyard that combines tradition and modernity, and so does its '94 product. Its aroma is majestic: we recognize berries, spices, pomegranate and hazelnut, all nuances that reappear on the palate. The power of the extracts and the impact of the tannins create exceptional texture.

91

Imported by Vias
New York, NY

TRENTINO PINOT GRIGIO RITRATTI '95

Cantina Sociale La Vis
Lavis [Trento]
tel. 39-461-246325

*T*he first Pinto Grigio ever to join the ranks of our Top Italian Wines is made by what is far and away the best cooperative winery in the Trentino region. This dazzlingly elegant white has a straw-yellow color with golden nuances and an intensely fruity aroma with tones of white peach and pear. On the palate it is full, smooth, long, and free of any acidic harshness.

90

Imported by Juno Importing
HoHoKus, NJ

ALTO ADIGE CABERNET SAUVIGNON MUMELTERHOF '94

Cantina Sociale
Santa Maddalena
Bolzano - tel. 39-471-972944

A real dark horse among the reds from the South Tyrol, Cabernet Mumelterhof '94 won a blind tasting hands down, over all its direct competitors. A splendid wine emerging from a winery that is clearly in a period of dramatic improvement. The color is a concentrated ruby, the aromas are intense and characteristic of this variety, with elegant fruity and herbaceous scents. The taste is rich, extremely full and long, its tannins velvety and compact.

94

Not imported

ALTO ADIGE
CABERNET SAUVIGNON
RISERVA '93

C. Viticoltori di Caldaro
Caldaro [Bolzano]
tel. 39-471-963149

*T*his is the second top ranking in a row for Cantina Sociale di Caldaro, again for its most representative red, this time in its '93 version. A wine with great impact, a very concentrated garnet ruby hue, and extremely elegant aromas with fruity tones, hints of vanilla and light herbaceous nuances. The flavor is full, still decidedly tannic, but well-supported by the impressive structure that determines an outstandingly long aftertaste.

93

Not imported

ALTO ADIGE LAGREIN SCURO
GRIESER PRESTIGE LINE
RISERVA '93

Cantina di Gries
Bolzano
tel. 39-471-270909

*T*his is the first time a Lagrein Scuro reaches and goes beyond our crucial 90-100 score. Produced by a winery known for this type of wine, it was chosen by the Bolzano Chamber of Commerce for its own 100th year anniversary celebration. The color is an impenetrable purplish ruby; there are intense aromas of blueberry, spice and vanilla. The flavor is concentrated, with compact tannins that are still a little aggressive due to the wine's extreme youth.

92

Not imported

ALTO ADIGE SAUVIGNON ST. VALENTIN '95

Cantina Sociale San Michele Appiano
Appiano [Bolzano]
tel. 39-471-664654

A seductive, fascinating wine, like a Marlene Dietrich come-hither-look. Its greatness lies in the exuberant, tropical, almost savage tones of its aroma. The color is a classic straw-yellow with green nuances. The scent is incredible: it has notes of mango, kiwi, ripe pineapple, and elderberry flowers, all intense and overwhelming. The experience is repeated in the assertive fullness of the flavor with an aftertaste that is a rerun of the aromatic richness of the scent.

Imported by Siena Imports
San Francisco, CA

ALTO ADIGE CABERNET LÖWENGANG '92

Alois Lageder
Bolzano
tel. 39-471-809500

A great return of Alois Lageder to the winners' ranks. He does it with a remarkable version of Cabernet Löwengang from the difficult '92 vintage. It is a splendidly concentrated color, an intense, garnet ruby. The scent is lightly herbaceous and mentholated with notes of raspberry and cassis. The full and elegant flavor reveals such exceptionally fine tannins that we needn't envy the wine's more famous cousins across the Alps.

Imported by Lauber Imports
New York, NY

ALTO ADIGE PINOT BIANCO WEISSHAUS '95

C. Produttori Colterenzio
Cornaiano [Bolzano]
tel. 39-471-664246

*A*delicious fruity, elegant Pinot Bianco that we could drink by the gallon. It is made by the cooperative winery, Cantina Produttori Colterenzio, an important, prestigious presence on the Alto Adige viticulture scene. The wine is a clear straw-yellow color with subtle golden highlights. The aroma is deliciously fragrant, with scents of banana and ripe pineapple. The taste is perfectly balanced, elegant and delicate.

90

Imported by Diamond Wine Merchants
Emeryville, CA

ALTO ADIGE PINOT NERO VILLA BARTHENAU VIGNA S. URBANO '93

Hofstätter
Termeno [Bolzano]
tel. 39-471-860161

*T*he king of Italian Pinot Nero reclaims the throne with this excellent version from the '93 vintage. Paolo Foradori and his son Martin are skilled in interpreting a variety that reveals its best qualities only in the hands of those who know their stuff, especially in the vineyard. Pinot Nero Vigna S. Urbano '93 is an intense garnet ruby color. Elegant aromas with notes of black currants and oak, a concentrated taste that is already quite balanced although still showing a slight edge of residual tannic and acid.

90

Imported by Vinifera Imports
Ronkonkoma, NY

IL ROSSO
DELL'ABAZIA '94

Serafini & Vidotto
Nervesa della Battaglia [Treviso]
tel. 39-422-773281

*F*rancesco Serafini and Antonello Vidotto, discouraged for a while by their difficult terrain, are finally seeing their efforts bear fruit. The most exciting result is this blend of Cabernet Sauvignon, Franc and Merlot: a concentrated ruby color with blue tinges; dense aromas of black fruits, hazelnuts, citrus fruit and aromatic herbs; exotic and fat in the mouth with very sweet tannins and an exciting and amazingly long finish.

96

Imported by Europvin S.A.
Bordeaux, France

RECIOTO CLASSICO
DELLA VALPOLICELLA
GIOVANNI ALLEGRINI '93

Allegrini
Fumane [Verona]
tel. 39-45-7701138

*R*ecioto Classico is certainly the most traditional wine of the Valpolicella. It is a sweet and very special red, with few peers in Italy. This '93, made by the Allegrini and named for the winery's founder, is one of the very best we have tasted in the last few years. It has a dark ruby color, scents of plum jam and pastry, and a fairly sweet taste that is both very full and very long.

93

Imported by Paterno
Chicago, IL

AMARONE CLASSICO '90

Allegrini
Fumane [Verona]
tel. 39-45-7701138

*I*mpressive and austere, as classic Amarone should be, especially one that comes from a good vintage like '90. An intense garnet color, it has very concentrated fragrance with scents of raisins, cherries preserved in spirits, and a hint of cocoa. The taste is full, not completely dry, and extremely long.

92

Imported by Paterno
Chicago, Il

PASSITO DELLA ROCCA '93

Leonildo Pieropan
Soave [Verona]
tel. 39-45-6190171

*M*ade from Riesling, Sauvignon, Trebbiano and Garganega grapes, this is a superb sweet wine that resembles a late harvest Alsatian in its balance and structure. It has a brilliant gold color and intense, elegant aromas with scents of pastry and caramelized fruit. The taste is delicately sweet, quite concentrated, and benefits from a barely perceptible brushstroke of pleasant acidity.

92

Imported by Empson USA
Alexandria, VA

VENETO

AMARONE '90

Corte Sant'Alda
Mezzane di Sotto [Verona]
tel. 39-45-8880006

*C*orte Sant'Alda makes its first appearance in our enological Olympus with its wonderful Amarone '90, an excellent year for this zone. It is an intense and concentrated garnet color, and has a very complex aroma with evident scents of cherries preserved in spirits. It is harmonious and rich on the palate with a light brushstroke of semi-sweetness in the background and an extremely long finish.

90

Imported by Alberico Wines
Haddonfield, NJ

VENETO

AMARONE VIGNETO DI MONTE LODOLETTA '89

Dal Forno
Illasi [Verona]
tel. 39-45-7834923

*T*his is the fourth time this winery, a new name among top quality producers, has broken the 90-100 barrier with its Amarone. It is a very powerful red even though it is from '89, an unexceptional year. A vivid and fairly concentrated garnet color, it has complex perfumes, less rustic than those in the past, but of astonishing intensity. It is soft and full in the mouth and has very good length.

90

Imported by Vias
New York, NY

PROSECCO
DI VALDOBBIADENE
SPUMANTE DRY GARNEI '95

Desiderio Bisol e Figli
Valdobbiadene [Treviso]
tel. 39-423-900552

*G*iving top ranking to a Prosecco may be pushing it a bit, but it rewards a very popular and Italianissimo wine that is often much better than many super-experts think. This Garnei di Bisol is a fragrant, fruity spumante with scents of wisteria and Golden Delicious apples. The flavor is lively, engaging, and the wine is very easy and pleasant to drink.

90

Not imported

PROSECCO
DI VALDOBBIADENE
SPUMANTE DRY S. STEFANO

VENETO

Ruggeri & C.
Valdobbiadene [Treviso]
tel. 39-423-975716

*N*ow we've gotten in the habit and are giving even a second top ranking to a Prosecco. Santo Stefano di Ruggeri is perhaps the most classic of them all. It is fragrant with scents of freshly-baked bread and fruit, has a good, full flavor with a pleasant acid vein on a very slightly semi-sweet background. It's worthwhile pointing out an enjoyable and amusing drink.

90

Imported by Villa Italia Inc.
South San Francisco, CA

31

SOAVE CLASSICO SUPERIORE CONTRADA SALVARENZA VIGNE VECCHIE '95

Gini
Monteforte d'Alpone [Verona]
tel. 39-45-7611908

*A*nother very Italian wine reaches the top ranks of our selections. This is a splendid Soave Classico aged in barriques and produced by Sandro Gini, one of the best producers of white wine in the Veneto. This one has a straw-yellow color with faint greenish highlights and delicately fruity aromas with hints of ripe fruit and vanilla. The taste is full and pronounced, and has a long finish.

90

Imported by Vindivino
Chicago, IL

COLLI OR. DEL FRIULI MERLOT '94

Miani
Buttrio [Udine]
tel. 39-432-674327

A knockout. We don't know how else to describe this sumptuous Friuli red, perhaps the region's biggest surprise this year. An almost opaque ruby color, with intense aromas of spice, oak, tobacco and berries. The taste explodes in the mouth. Its tannins are still quite present and its structure is a prizewinner. Superb.

94

Imported by Europvin S.A.
Bordeaux, France

FERRARI.
QUESTIONE DI ETICHETTA.

Occasions change,
the taste of tradition remains:
Ferrari Spumante,
from 1902, putting bubbles
where they count.

FERRARI
F.lli Lunelli s.p.a.

38040 Trento
via del Ponte di Ravina, 15 Italy
tel. +39 461 972 311 fax +39 461 913 008
e-mail: fertal@mbox.vol.it

THE FERRARI CELLARS, WE LOOK FORWARD TO YOU VISIT.
Brian Larky - Sole U.S. Agent - Ferrari USA
T (707) 257 7453 - F (707) 257 7527 e-mail: vinified@aol.com
Internet: WWW.spumante.it - alias talento.it.

MASSOLINO WINES SPOTLIGHT TH
NEBBIOLO TRUTH

WISDOM, TRADITION, EXPERIENCE, ENTHUSIASM c
together in this family-run winery located in Serralunga d'Alb
noble little village tucked away in the heart of the Barolo reg
The dedication and skills of four generations of the Massolino fa
have gone into the making and enhancement of their selected wi
Each wine from the vineyards on their «Vigna Rionda» estate is ble
with its own distinctive and magnificent nuances, the happy outc
of a 100 years quest for excellence:

BAROLO VIGNA RIONDA

BAROLO VIGNA PARAFADA

BAROLO VIGNA MARGHER

DOLCETTO VIGNA BARILO

BARBERA VIGNA MARGHE

MOSCATO D'ASTI

MASSOLINO
wine producers since 1896.

A very
greaT
pleasure

PinoT
Blanc

Weisshaus

COLTERENZIO

APPIANO - ITALY • TEL 04 71 / 66 42 46 • FAX 04 71 / 66 06 33

DUCA ENRICO

A Tradition of Winemaking Excellence

3 GLASSES-Gambero Rosso
1984, 1985, 1986, 1987
1988, 1990, 1992

RATED 95-*Wine & Spirit* Magazine
"Stars at amazing and gets better."

HIGHLY RECOMMENDED
The Wine Spectator

★★★★**FIRST RATE RED**
Restaurant Wine

GOLD MEDAL
Vinexpo Bordeaux 1986

GOLD MEDAL
Vinitaly 1993, 1996

COLLIO CHARDONNAY '94

La Castellada
Gorizia
tel. 39-481-33670

*T*he Chardonnay made this year by the Bensa brothers, owners of La Castellada winery, is an extraordinarily powerful white. Its hefty structure and rich concentration mean that it is still closed and compressed. The color is a lively golden straw-yellow, while the nose is generous, with complex scents of vanilla, roasting coffee, ripe fruit, and a background note of peanut butter. The taste is remarkably full and textured, with an exceptionally long finish.

92

Imported by Estate Wines
San Rafael, CA

COLLIO
TOCAI FRIULANO '95

Schiopetto
Capriva del Friuli [Gorizia]
tel. 39-481-80332

*M*ario Schiopetto's classic. A great Tocai again this year, even better than those wonderful ones from '93 and '94. It has a straw-yellow hue with light gold tinges. The aroma is generously fruity and complex, with traces of Williams pears and chocolate-covered mints. In the mouth it is full, well-defined and powerful, with a delicately bitterish finish and persistence worthy of the great wine that it is.

92

Imported by Winebow
HoHoKus, NJ

COLLIO
TOCAI FRIULANO '95

Villa Russiz
Capriva del Friuli [Gorizia]
tel. 39-481-80047

ianni Menotti returns to his whites after winning recognition for his Merlot Graf de La Tour last year. He does it with a classic Tocai '95, which we liked even more than his Sauvignon and Pinot Bianco, both excellent. This wine has a clear straw-yellow color and characteristic aromas with herbaceous and fruity notes, and very evident hints of peach. The taste is full, shows excellent structure, and is harmonious and persistent.

92

Imported by Empson USA
Alexandria, VA

ISONZO
TOCAI FRIULANO '95

Ronco del Gelso
Cormons [Gorizia]
tel. 39-481-61310

op quality wine is made in the vineyard. Just ask Giorgio Badin, a young grower from Isonzo. Some people claim to have heard him actually talking to his vines. The result is wines like this Tocai '95. It has a golden color with greenish tinges and a complex aroma with suggestions of peach and fresh walnuts. The flavor is downright explosive. Supple, concentrated, full-bodied, long: truly a unique wine. It comes from a grape that generally does not attain such a high level.

92

Not imported

RONCO
DELLE ACACIE '93

Abbazia di Rosazzo
Manzano [Udine]
tel. 39-432-759693

*T*his first appearance of Ronco delle Acacie in the top roster should be a more newsworthy story than the difficulties that the Abbazia di Rosazzo winery is facing.This '93 white, aged in barriques, was made from Chardonnay grapes with the addition of Pinot Bianco and Tocai. It is the best ever. The aromas are particularly elegant and well-expressed, with perfectly fused notes of vanilla and fruit. The flavor shows its characteristic fullness, but the wine is easier to drink.

92

Imported by Winebow
HoHoKus, NJ

VINTAGE TUNINA '94

Vinnaioli Jermann
Farra d'Isonzo [Gorizia]
tel. 39-481-888080

*T*he specialty of Silvio Jermann's winery is still Vintage Tunina. The '94 version is worthy of the laurels awarded its predecessors. As always, it is made from Chardonnay and Sauvignon grapes, with small amounts of Malvasia, Ribolla, Tocai, Pinot Bianco and Picolit. It has a slightly greenish straw color and is intensely fruity on the nose, with elegant aromas of white peach and apple. Offering great freshness, the flavor has the richness and length of the best years, with a hint of sweetness finely balanced by acidity.

92

Imported by Empson USA
Alexandria, VA

CHARDONNAY '94

Edi Kante
Duino - Aurisina [Trieste]
tel. 39-40-200761

*E*di Kante returns to our roster with a very impressive Chardonnay aged in barriques. Made from grapes coming from his miniscule vineyard near Trieste, it has a lightly gold-tinged straw-yellow color and an elegant, delicate nose with aromas of vanilla and ripe fruit. The taste is full, very balanced, and full of subtle nuances.

91

Imported by Winebow
HoHoKus, NJ

COLLI OR. DEL FRIULI PICOLIT '95

Girolamo Dorigo
Buttrio [Udine]
tel. 39-432-674268

*W*e never liked Picolit very much. We always thought it was overrated and far from being the Italian answer to the great Sauternes. Then we came across this marvelous wine made by Girolamo and Rosetta Dorigo and all our prejudices disappeared. This is a Picolit Passito, made from late harvest grapes, just the way Conte Asquini did it more than a century ago. It has an intense gold color and overwhelming aromas with notes of pastry and vanilla. The taste is sweet, full, fascinating. A little masterpiece.

91

Imported by Vinifera Imports
Ronkonkoma, NY

BIANCO DELLA CASTELLADA '94

La Castellada
Gorizia
tel. 39-481-33670

*T*his is a very unusual white, made from a blend of Tocai Friulano and Pinot Grigio aged in barriques with the addition of small quantities - about 20% - of Sauvignon and Ribolla. La Castellada winery is in the heart of Collio Goriziano. The '94 version is an intense and brilliant straw-yellow. The nose is characterized by intense notes of fruit and vanilla. In the mouth, the taste is full, very concentrated and long, although it still shows some lack of balance due to the wine's youth.

90

Imported by Estate Wines
San Rafael, CA

COLLIO PINOT BIANCO '95

Doro Princic
Cormons [Gorizia]
tel. 39-481-60723

*T*he best Pinot Bianco made in Friuli is produced by Princic just outside the town of Cormons in the heart of Collio. It has a clear, brilliant straw-yellow color and a nose that is characteristic of this grape variety, with faint aromas of fresh almonds and bananas. The flavor is delicately harmonious and free of harshness with an unexpectedly long finish.

90

Imported by Winebow
HoHoKus, NJ

COLLIO
TOCAI FRIULANO '95

Edi Keber
Cormons [Gorizia]
tel. 39-481-61184

*A*lthough he is famous for producing very affordable wines, this year Edi Keber showed us that top quality Friuli wine is also within his reach. His Tocai '95 is a little jewel. It has a gold-tinged straw-yellow color and an intense, characteristic nose, with notes of white peach and fresh walnuts. The flavor is full, well-defined, and has a subtle, elegant bitterish aftertaste.

90

Imported by Viva Vino Import
Eddystone, PA

COLLI OR. DEL FRIULI
VERDUZZO FRIULANO
CASALI GODIA '94

Livon
San Giovanni al Natisone [Udine]
tel. 39-432-757173

*I*f there is one producer that everyone in Friuli agrees is taking giant steps towards improving his wines, it's Tonino Livon. We are very happy to be able to include him in our highest category. The honor goes to a very unusual, fascinating wine, an elegant, almost completely dry Verduzzo Friulano. It has a golden straw color and a supple, refined, entrancing taste.

90

Imported by Angelini Wine Ltd.
New London, CT

ISONZO CHARDONNAY
CIAMPAGNIS VIERIS '94

Vie di Romans
Mariano del Friuli [Gorizia]
tel. 39-481-69600

*T*he undisputed champion of Sauvignon, Gianfranco Gallo, wins plaudits this year for a splendid Chardonnay. We don't know how he'll feel about this, but the fact is that this is a very interesting wine, and particularly well-made. It has a golden straw color and aromas in which scents of vanilla blend well with the fruity fragrances of the varietal. The flavor is full, powerful, structured, and has excellent length.

90

Exported by MarcDe Grazia
Florence, Italy

MONTSCLAPADE '92

Girolamo Dorigo
Buttrio [Udine]
tel. 39-432-674268

A classic Bordeaux blend from Cabernet Sauvignon, Cabernet Franc and Merlot grapes. Despite an uninspiring year, it displays a dark and concentrated ruby color and is very elegant on the nose with complex and aristocratic notes of berries, spices and cocoa. On the palate it is extremely powerful with sweet tannins and remarkable length.

90

Imported by Vinifera Imports
Ronkonkoma, NY

SIEPI '94

Castello di Fonterutoli
Castellina in Chianti [Siena]
tel. 39-577-740309

*S*imply delicious. It is made from the best Sangiovese grapes with the addition of small amounts of Merlot. It is an extraordinarily supple red, easy to drink and powerful at the same time. It has a dark and concentrated ruby color, intensely fruity aromas with scents of black currants, sour cherries and tobacco. The taste is impressive: very balanced but also very concentrated and persistent, without any tannic or acidic harshness. In other words, a champion.

96

Imported by Empson USA
Alexandria, VA

VIGNA L'APPARITA MERLOT '92

Castello di Ama
Gaiole in Chianti [Siena]
tel. 39-577-746031

A great red with Tuscan character but an international accent. Absolutely one of the best Italian wines, and one of the best Merlots in the world, including Pomerol. It is a very intense and concentrated ruby color. The bouquet is most elegant, with aromas of tobacco, sour cherry, vanilla and graphite on a fruity background with hints of sour cherry and currants. On the palate, the wine has remarkable body, well-supported by sweet tannin which creates an almost magical balance.

96

Imported by Vindivino
Chicago, IL

CHIANTI CLASSICO
RANCIA RISERVA '93

Fattoria di Felsina
Castelnuovo Berardenga [Siena]
tel. 39-577-355117

*O*nce again, it's the best of its year. Perfectly made by Giuseppe Mazzocolin, the firm's head, and Franco Bernabei, one of the best-known Italian winemakers, Rancia '93 is less powerful and concentrated than the unforgettable '90 vintage, but, as usual, it is exceptional. It is an intense ruby color, and has elegant aromas with notes of berries, wet earth and vanilla, and a full, powerful taste, good length and particularly fine tannins.

Imported by Vinifera Imports
Ronkonkoma, NY

MAESTRO RARO '91

Fattoria di Felsina
Castelnuovo Berardenga [Siena]
tel. 39-577-355117

*W*e really didn't expect this. A great Cabernet Sauvignon produced by Felsina, the reigning king of Sangiovese. Maestro Raro comes from the '91 vintage, which in general was only fair. It shows such impressive concentration that it leaves all its competitors in the dust. The wine is an extremely concentrated garnet ruby color, with aromas of ripe fruit and vanilla. The tones of the terroir clearly prevail over those that are varietal. The taste is so rich that it rounds out all possible tannic harshness.

Imported by Vinifera Imports
Ronkonkoma, NY

MASSETO '93

Tenuta dell'Ornellaia
Bolgheri [Livorno]
tel. 39-565-762140

*W*e had never given top ranking to any wines from Lodovico Antinori's Ornellaia winery, but this year we applaud two. The most convincing wine is Masseto '93, a splendid red made solely from Merlot grapes. It has an intense ruby color with flickering garnet highlights. The aromas are characteristic of this grape and express fruity and herbaceous tones with notes of sour cherries, tobacco and, further back, sage. The taste is supple and compact, with very sweet tannins and spectacular length.

95

Imported by Kobrand
New York, NY

BRUNELLO
DI MONTALCINO
SCHIENA D'ASINO '90

Mastrojanni
Montalcino [Siena]
tel. 39-577-835681

*A*fter the success of its Riserva '88 and Brunello '90, Mastrojanni makes it a triple with Brunello Schiena d'Asino '90. The color is an intense ruby, and the bouquet is very concentrated: berries and morello cherries against a background of spicy wood. In the mouth, the strength of the tannins and the assertiveness of the alcohol is balanced, as is the sensation of pleasantness and concentration. The length is long and substantial, as with any great Brunello.

94

Imported by Selected Estates of Europe
Mamaronek, NY

CONCERTO '93

Castello di Fonterutoli
Castellina in Chianti [Siena]
tel. 39-577-740309

*A*round, harmonious wine, a true masterpiece of elegant and aristocratic tones. Made, as always, from Sangiovese grapes with the addition of small amounts of Cabernet Sauvignon, this year is probably its best ever. The color is a very intense and concentrated ruby, its fruity aromas are intense and elegant, with notes of raspberry and sour cherry against a light brush stroke of vanilla. On the palate, the wine reveals harmony unusual for a Sangiovese red, with no harshness and excellent length.

94

Imported by Empson USA
Alexandria, VA

CORTACCIO '93

Villa Cafaggio
Greve in Chianti [Siena]
tel. 39-55-8549094

*V*illa Cafaggio's Stefano Farkas deserves our applause. Above all because he is convinced that everything depends on the quality of the grape. His Cortaccio '93 is an impressively powerful red made of Cabernet Sauvignon grapes. It has a dark and very concentrated ruby color. Its nose is intense, with scents of red fruits (blackberries, raspberries, currants) and light, toasty, vanilla tones. The taste has great impact, with tannins in evidence but well-sustained by the wine's structure.

94

Imported by Fine Wines International Inc.
Rutherford, NJ

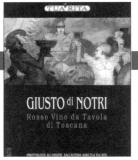

GIUSTO DI NOTRI '94

Tua Rita
Suvereto [Livorno]
tel. 39-565-829237

*T*he '93 version almost reached ninety points, and Giusto di Notri '94 left that score far behind. An impressive red made of Cabernet Sauvignon and Merlot, it comes from a zone that pioneers top quality winemaking, on the border between the provinces of Livorno and Grosseto. It has a deep and intense ruby color, balsamic aromas with mentholated tones, and notes of sage and eucalyptus. The flavor is full, supple, and without any excessive harshness, even if the tannins have not completely evolved.

94

Not imported

CHIANTI CLASSICO RISERVA '93

Casa Emma
Barberino Val d'Elsa [Firenze]
tel. 39-55-8072859

*T*his beautiful little winery in the Barberino Val d'Elsa zone appears among our winners for the first time. It debuts with a sumptuous Chianti Classico Riserva '93, elegant and concentrated at the same time, made from a vintage that gave some interesting results in that particular sub-zone. A great red, with a remarkably dense purplish ruby color. The aromas are intensely fruity with notes of blackberry, raspberry and vanilla, while the taste is full, well-defined, and still fairly tannic.

93

Imported by Elizabeth Imports
Denver, CO

SASSICAIA '93

Tenuta San Guido
Bolgheri [Livorno]
tel. 39-565-762003

*E*xploiting an excellent vintage, Sassicaia, Italy's flagship wine, presents one of its most enthralling versions of the last few years. It is compact and powerful right from its dark and impenetrable ruby color. Its nose shows intense aromas, rich in scents of berries, cocoa, and vanilla. On the palate, the wine has classic elegance and balance and is supple, very rich in fruit, and characterized by important tannins and incredible finesse.

93

Imported by Kobrand
New York, NY

CHIANTI CLASSICO
GIORGIO PRIMO '94

La Massa
Greve in Chianti [Firenze]
tel. 39-55-852701

*L*ast year's big surprise. This time, the wine confirms its extraordinary potential in an exceptional '94 version. The 20 hectare (50 acres) estate where it is made is located in the heart of the Conca d'Oro of Panzano. It is a lively and intense ruby color. The aromas are delicately fruity, with elegant notes of sour cherries and violets. The taste is supple and concentrated, and expresses excellent body, but also remarkable balance and smooth, noble tannins.

92

Imported by Martin Scott Wines
Lake Success, NY

IL PARETO '93

Tenuta di Nozzole
Greve in Chianti [Firenze]
tel. 39-55-858018

*T*his fantastic Cabernet Sauvignon from Nozzole never disappoints us. The '93 version, even if it doesn't have the amazing power of the '88 and '90, shows impressive character and elegance. It displays a very concentrated and intense ruby color, and its bouquet is partly fruity and partly balsamic, with notes of graphite, spice and berries against a delicate toasty background. The wine makes a memorable impact on the palate with its full and tannic flavor.

Imported by Kobrand
New York, NY

BRUNELLO
DI MONTALCINO
RISERVA '90

Capanna di Cencioni
Montalcino [Siena]
tel. 39-577-848298

A great traditional Brunello, but without the excesses or the naiveté that these wines often present. A very interesting Brunello Riserva '90, it is produced by Patrizio Cencioni, whose winery is considered among the most classic in the zone. The wine has a garnet ruby color, evolved fruity aromas with notes of sour cherries and kirsch, and a well-defined, powerful taste, still somewhat tannic.

Imported by Masciarelli Wine
Cohasset, MA

BRUNELLO DI MONTALCINO RISERVA '90

Castelgiocondo
Montalcino [Siena]
tel. 39-577-848492

*C*astelgiocondo has taken giant steps since it came under the control of Marchesi de' Frescobaldi. So many, in fact, that a wine genius like Robert Mondavi chose this winery for his second joint venture after the one that led to the production of Opus One with the Rothschilds. It's certain that this year's Brunello Riserva '90 will be an essential point of reference for those produced in the future. It has concentrated, generous, and elegant berry aromas, and it is harmonious, well-structured and impressive on the palate.

91

Imported by Paterno
Chicago, IL

VINO NOBILE DI MONTEPULCIANO VIGNA DELL'ASINONE '93

Poliziano
Montepulciano [Siena]
tel. 39-578-738171

*B*y giving up its status as a Riserva, this Vigna dell'Asinone '93 was able to come on the market this year, getting the jump on a large number of Vino Nobile Riserva '93 labels not available until the middle of '97. This is a very respectable version; the '93 vintage in Montepulciano was almost at the level of the '90. It displays a dark ruby color and already has some garnet tinges. The aroma is intense, with scents of sour cherries and new oak. The taste is full, still generously tannic, and quite long.

91

Imported by Vinifera Imports
Ronkonkoma, NY

TUSCANY

BRUNELLO DI MONTALCINO POGGIO ALL'ORO RISERVA '90

Castello Banfi
Montalcino [Siena]
tel. 39-577-840111

*T*he salient characteristics of Banfi wines are high standards and reliability that few firms can match. Poggio all'Oro, a Riserva di Brunello '90, is an excellent example of how pleasantness can co-exist with structure. It has an intense ruby color and notable aromas of berries, with discernible scents of morello cherries. Although easy on the palate, at the same time it is concentrated and velvety. Should be cellared a bit longer.

90

Imported by Banfi Products Corp.
Old Brookville, NY

TUSCANY

BRUNELLO DI MONTALCINO VIGNA DEL LAGO '90

Val di Suga
Montalcino [Siena]
tel. 39-577-848701

*T*his is the most balanced and elegant among the Brunellos honored this year. It comes from the northeastern part of the zone, where the wines have exactly these characteristics. It displays an intense, concentrated garnet ruby color. The aroma is fruity, elegant and has refined hints of vanilla and berries. The taste, as we mentioned, is particularly harmonious with a very fine and velvety tannic texture.

90

Imported by Wilson Daniels Ltd.
St. Helena, CA

ORNELLAIA '93

Tenuta dell'Ornellaia
Bolgheri [Livorno]
tel. 39-565-762140

*A*fter a long slow march that lasted for many years, Ornellaia finally crosses the ninety points frontier with the excellent '93 vintage. Lodovico Antinori and enologist Tibor Gal offer us a dark ruby-hued wine with purplish tinges. The nose opens with a rich display of scents that range from berries to herbaceous, with elegant notes of smoke and vanilla. On the palate the wine is potent, fine and structured, rich in fruit and elegant tannins, complex and very long. To sum it up: a great wine.

90

Imported by Kobrand
New York, NY

TIGNANELLO '93

TUSCANY

Marchesi Antinori
Firenze
tel. 39-55-23595

*T*ignanello's return to the ranks of the nineties is important news. This wine wrote the history of Italian enology of the last 25 years and is the only one that enjoys a production capacity of more than 300,000 bottles. Made from Sangiovese [75%] and Cabernet Sauvignon [25%], in its '93 version it displays a concentrated garnet ruby color. Its fragrance is of ripe berries, with a delicate vanilla note. The structure is satisfying on the palate with a smooth taste and excellent balance.

90

Imported by Remy Amerique Inc.
New York, NY

49

ROSSO CONERO
DORICO '93

Alessandro Moroder
Ancona
tel. 39-71-898232

*A*n old friend is back in the ranks of Top Italian Wines. Alessandro Moroder's Dorico in its '93 version benefits from the technical expertise of Franco Bernabei, supreme and ubiquitous wine consultant. Made solely from Montepulciano grapes, the wine displays an intense, almost impenetrable ruby color. The nose has distinct aromas of berries and vanilla; the taste is full, supple and long.

93

Imported by Vinifera Imports
Ronkonkoma, NY

VERDICCHIO
DEI CASTELLI DI JESI CLASSICO
CONTRADA BALCIANA '94

Sartarelli
Montecarotto [Ancona]
tel. 39-731-89732

*W*e're going out on a limb. This is the greatest Verdicchio of all time. Made with slightly over-ripe grapes, it displays a rather bright straw-yellow color and very interesting and original aromas. The nose has fruity and mineral tones, approximating the tonalities of a late-harvest Riesling. The taste is concentrated, quite supple and very long, with an insistent bitterish aftertaste that is very pleasing.

93

Imported by Vias
New York, NY

AKRONTE CABERNET '93

Boccadigabbia
Civitanova Marche [Macerata]
tel. 39-733-70728

*E*ven if this wine has some rough edges, hallelujah, finally a
red with real character. It has an extremely concentrated and very
intense ruby color. The perfumes are also intense, varietal, and a
little rustic with notes of berries and oak. The flavor is full, tannic,
well-defined, and has a pleasant, slightly bitter aftertaste. A really
wonderful wine.

91

Imported by Michael Skurnik Wines
Syosset, NY

MIRUM '94

La Monacesca
Civitanova Marche [Macerata]
tel. 39-733-812602

*M*ade from over-ripe Verdicchio grapes from the heart of the
the Matelica zone. With this version, the wine has changed name
from Mirus to Mirum. By any name, it is still the result of the
experiments carried out by young Aldo Cifola, owner of La
Monacesca winery. Mirum '94 has an intense straw-yellow color.
Its nose is delicately fruity, with notes of plum and medlar. The
taste is well-defined and notably long, with a pleasantly acidic
note throughout and a slightly bitter aftertaste on the finish.

90

Imported by Tricana Imports Inc.
Plainview, NJ

SAGRANTINO DI MONTEFALCO 25 ANNI '93

Arnaldo Caprai - Val di Maggio
Montefalco [Perugia]
tel. 39-742-378802

*W*e thought of the rumbling of thunder while we were tasting this extraordinary Umbrian red. That's what it was like. We have rarely tasted such a concentrated wine in all our years on the tasting trail. The color was an impenetrable dark ruby, the bouquet was incredibly intense and the taste so dense and persistent that it was difficult to isolate and analyze its various components. This wine will evolve for decades, reaching peaks of complexity that are unthinkable now.

97

Imported by Villa Italia Inc.
South San Francisco, CA

CERVARO DELLA SALA '94

Castello della Sala
Ficulle [Terni]
tel. 39-763-86051

*T*he Castello della Sala estate is owned by the Marchesi Antinori and is under the management of Albiera Antinori with the guidance of Renzo Cotarella, one of Italy's leading young enologists. The best wine they produce is this Cervaro della Sala, a white aged in barriques and made from Chardonnay (80%) and Grechetto (20%). The '92 version displays an intense straw-yellow with golden highlights. The rich aromas are of ripe fruit and vanilla. On the palate, the wine is full-flavored, balanced, and very long.

94

Imported by Remy Amerique Inc.
New York, NY

MONTIANO '94

Cantina Falesco
Montefiascone [Viterbo]
tel. 39-761-827032

*T*hree cheers for Riccardo Cotarella, the great winemaker of central Italy and technical consultant to many wineries that, with his help, manage to squeeze blood out of turnips. He also makes some wines for his own winery, Falesco, among which is this Montiano, made solely of Merlot grapes. The '94 is his best ever, even better than the '93. The color is an intense ruby, the aromas are deliciously fruity and elegant, and the taste is full-bodied, with particularly fine-grained tannins.

90

Imported by Winebow
HoHoKus, NJ

TREBBIANO D'ABRUZZO '92

Edoardo Valentini
Loreto Aprutino [Pescara]
tel. 39-85-8291138

*T*he wizard is working his magic again with this Trebbiano '92. Edoardo Valentini offers us an impressive white that in spite of a disastrous harvest everywhere, shows its true aristocratic colors. A distinct golden straw-yellow, it has a veil of fizziness that disappears immediately in the glass. The nose is complex and evolved, with hints of yeast, ripe fruit and herbaceous notes. On the palate it is full, concentrated, and very long.

90

Imported by Vinifera Imports
Ronkonkoma, NY

CHARDONNAY '94

Tasca d'Almerita - Regaleali
Sclafani Bagni [Palermo]
tel. 39-921-542522

*F*ourth winning year in a row for a wine that gets better with each version. The yield in its vineyard of origin rarely exceeds 35 quintals (7700 pounds) per hectare (2.46 acres). It has a generous, intense, spicy, varietal bouquet with a note of vanilla that comes from the wood. The taste is fat, supple and structured, with a seemingly endless finish. To appreciate its very special character, its power, elegance, and drinkability, sip it on its own, very, very slowly.

93

Imported by Winebow
HoHoKus, NJ

DUCA ENRICO '92

Duca di Salaparuta - Vini Corvo
Casteldaccia [Palermo]
tel. 39-91-953988

*D*uca di Salaparuta, producing over ten million bottles, has always been Sicilian wine's best ambassador. Duca Enrico is made from Nero d'Avola grapes grown in central-western Sicily in hillside vineyards. The yields are very limited, 40 quintals (8800 pounds) a hectare (2.47 acres). The color is a bright ruby and the aromas are rich and spicy with notes of plums and blackberries. On the palate the wine is supple and has sweet tannins, juicy concentration, and great length.

90

Imported by Paterno
Chicago, IL

MOSCATO PASSITO DI PANTELLERIA MARTINGANA '93

Salvatore Murana
Pantelleria [Trapani]
tel. 39-923-915231

*S*alvatore Murana is the king of Moscato di Pantelleria. This time his wine is one of the best in the country. Moscato Passito di Pantelleria Martingana '93 is nectar for the gods. It has an intense amber color and entrancing aromas, with notes of dried fruit (apricots and dates) and fig jam. The taste is sweet, very concentrated, and has an aftertaste on the finish that reiterates all the initial aromas.

90

Imported by Premium Brands Inc.
Forest Hills, NY

TURRIGA '91

Antonio Argiolas
Serdiana [Cagliari]
tel. 39-70-740606

*T*urriga is a great Sardinian red. It is made from Cannonau, Carignano, Sangiovese and Malvasia Nera grapes, and aged for 18 months in small casks of French wood. The wine is bottle-aged for another eight to ten months. It is a dark, very concentrated ruby color, with intense and persistent aromas of berries preserved in spirits, with a note of vanilla in the background. The taste is very concentrated and smooth, and the long finish has a very pleasant return to the taste of berries.

90

Imported by Winebow
HoHoKus, NJ

AFTERWORD

During Gambero Rosso's two years on American newsstands, we have presented the year's top scorers three times. We have also published many special articles on Italian wine.

Other major features about wine have been:

BRUNELLO DI MONTALCINO *(no. 2, 1995)*

- The Importance of being Brunello
- The Sommelier's Corner
- Beyond Brunello : Moscadello and Rosso di Montalcino
- Montalcino: Not only Wine
- Montalcino: Walking the Mouse Trail
- The Wineries of Montalcino
- The Century According to Biondi Santi: a vertical tasting
- Biondi Santi: The Story
- Where to stop, where to shop
- House rental

CHIANTI *(no. 3, 1995)*

- Chianti Classico: The Next Generation
- Renaissance Farmhouse: Hotel Belvedere San Leonino

- Olive Oil: Liquid Gold in the Hills of Chianti
- Wine Routes: Five Itineraries in Chianti
- The Estates of Chianti Classico
- Medici Ceramics for Modern Tables

SASSICAIA   *(no. 4, 1995)*

- Gold Star over Bolgheri: Sassicaia DOC
- Giacomo Tachis: Winemaker Tells All
- Tasting Notes: Sassicaia 1992-1968

BAROLO GRAN BUSSIA   *(no. 6, 1995)*

- A Cult Barolo
- The Courteous Innovator: Interview with Aldo Conterno
- Barolo Gran Bussia: A Tasting

MERLOT L'APPARITA   *(no. 7, 1995)*

- The Matchless Merlot
- The Protagonists: Castello di Ama
- L' Apparita: A Tasting

THE WINES OF VERONA   *(no. 7, 1995)*

- Lake Garda: Accidentally Mediterranean
- Foresteria Serègo Alighieri: A Stay in the Country

Gambero Rosso is not only a magazine about wine. We also offer our readers accurate and up-to-date information about travel in Italy. Some is about wine regions - all of the sections above are packed with suggestions for hotels, restaurants, places to go. Other specials are about ways to avoid the crowds and see the best; our ideas for off beat, off season travel.

TUSCANY: DISCOVERING THE LITTLE BIG PLACES   *(no. 1, 1995)*

- The Etruscan Wines
    A close-up look at the prized vineyards and top winemakers around the little town of Bolgheri
- There's a Small Hotel
    San Sepolcro's L'Oroscopo : a verdant inn and the sublime Piero della Francesca
- Exploring the Byways: Food, Shelter and Shopping
  A House of One's Own
    Chianti: four luminous houses to rent in Fonterutoli, Paneretta, Volpaia and Poggerino
- Two Tuscan Recipes to Remember

ROME: A NEW LOOK AT THE OLD CITY   *(no. 2, 1995)*

- Rome at Your Feet
    Five walks to find a Rome of your own. Restaurants and cafés that make every mouthful matter.
- Around Campo de'Fiori
- Strolling the Ghetto
- Wandering in Trastevere

- Exploring the Forum
- Seeing Caravaggio
- Paying your Respects to Papal Rome
- Turning Back the Clock: Hotel Locarno
- Where to stay: Hotels
- Rome's best hotel, buys and restaurants
  from the Gambero Rosso guide to Rome

CAPRI AND THE AMALFI COAST: SKIPPING OVER THE WATER *(no. 3, 1995)*

- Capri and the Amalfi Coast: Getting Around by Sea
  *Avoiding the crowds in the Mediterranean's
  prettiest places.*
- Food, Shelter, and Shopping in Naples and Sorrento
- The Wines of Campania
- Capri: Following your Feet
- Positano: Life on the Vertical
- Amalfi: Sovereign of the Sea
- Ravello: The Seduction of the South
- Limoncello: Yellow Nectar from the Blue Isle

TUSCANY: JEWEL BOX CITIES, RUSTIC RETREATS *(no. 4, 1995)*

- Pisa Abandoned by the Sea
- Lodging, Food and Shopping in Pisa
- Lucca Within the Walls
- Lodging, Food and Shopping in Lucca
- The Villas of Lucca Outside the Walls
- Montecarlo di Lucca
  A Simple inn in a Small Town
- The Garfagnana Green Hills
- Grotta del Vento Into the Deep
- Farro: A Grain from the Past
- Lodging and Food in the Garfagnana

*Back copies of Gambero Rosso
may be ordered from Speedimpex, USA Inc
(1-800-969-1268)*

CASTELLO DI FARNETELLA

CHIANTI

CASTELLO DI FARNETELLA - SINALUNGA (SIENA) ITALIA

CASTELLO DI FONTERUTOLI

[...] E DÉ DARE, A DÌ
16 DICEMBRE (1398)
FIORINI 3 SOLDI 26 DENARI 8
A PIETRO DI TINO RICCIO
PER BARILI 6
DI VINO DI CHIANTI...,
LI DETTI PAGHAMO
PER LETTERA DI
SER LAPO MAZZEI [...]

THE DATINI ARCHIVES
THE FIRST OFFICIAL DOCUMENT WHICH
MENTIONS CHIANTI WINE

[...]. I THANK YOU FOR YOUR
OBLIGING ACCT.
OF THE CULTURE OF THE VINE,
AND AM HAPPY TO HEAR
THAT YOUR PLANTATION
OF THEM IS IN
SO PROSPEROUS A WAY [...]

GEORGE WASHINGTON TO FILIPPO MAZZEI
NEW WINDSOR, JULY 1ST 1779

[...]. NON VI CURATE DELLA SPESA
DI QUEL VINO;
CHE, BENCH'EGLI FOSSE CARO,
LA BONTÀ RISTORA: [...]

SER LAPO MAZZEI
FLORENCE, APRIL 29TH 1394

MAZZEI
IN FONTERUTOLI SINCE 1435

INDEX

Gambero Rosso Tells All